Let's Sort TEXTURE

KIM THOMPSON

TABLE OF CONTENTS

A Pelican Book

SEAHORSE PUBLISHING

Teaching Tips for Caregivers and Teachers:

Research shows that one of the best ways for students to learn a new topic is to read about it.

Before Reading

- Read the title and predict what the book will be about.
- Read the "Words to Know" and discuss the meaning of each word.
- Read the back cover to see what the book is about.

During Reading

- When a student gets to a word that is unknown, ask them to look at the rest of the sentence to find clues to help with the meaning of the unknown word.
- Motivate students with praise and encouragement.

After Reading

- Discuss the main idea of the book.
- Ask students to give one detail that they learned in the book.

SIGHT WORDS

can
make
these
this
to
use
you

Words to Know

feel

prickly

fuzzy

rough

groups

smooth

You can **feel**.

You can use feel to make **groups**.

groups

This group feels **smooth**.

This group feels **rough**.

This group feels **fuzzy**.

This group feels **prickly**.

Can you group these?

Count the items on page 15.
How many groups have 4?
How many groups have 6?

Index

Written by: Kim Thompson
Design by: Jen Bowers
Series Development: James Earley

Photos: Shutterstock.com/cover: border top ©2019 Cristina Ionescu, border bottom ©2018 3d_kot, images: ©2013 John Brueske, ©2021 NIKCOA, ©2016 CoffeeChocolates, ©2018 Dzha33; p.3 & 4 ©2021 Ksenia Shestakova; p.7 ©2018 Pineapple studio, ©2017 Serebryakova Ekaterina, ©2016 irin-k, ©2019 Maks Narodenko, ©2019 VITTO-STUDIO; p.9 ©2016 Cabeca de Marmore, ©2013 Sarah2, ©2012 JDCarballo, p.11 ©2017 Yellow Cat, ©2017 effective stock photos, ©2013 Eric Isselee, ©2018 3drenderings; p.13 ©2011 photossee, ©2018 Pineapple studio, ©2020 ChameleonsEye; p.14 ©2011 Tsekhmister, ©2019 Doubleclix, ©2008 Sebastian Knight, ©2019 PixaHub

Library of Congress PCN Data
Texture /Kim Thompson
Let's Sort
ISBN 978-1-6389-7957-9 (hard cover)
ISBN 979-8-8873-5016-5 (paperback)
ISBN 979-8-8873-5075-2 (EPUB)
ISBN 979-8-8873-5134-6 (eBook)
Library of Congress Control Number: 2022942698

Printed in the United States of America.

Seahorse Publishing Company
www.seahorsepub.com

Published in the United States
Seahorse Publishing
PO Box 771325
Coral Springs, FL 33077

SEAHORSE PUBLISHING